Vikings

Contents	Page
Long ago	2-3
Longships	4-5
Raiders	6-7
Weapons	8-9
Traders	10-11
Homes	12-13
Family fun	14-15
Gods	16

written by John Lockyer

The Vikings lived more than 2,000 years ago. Their homes were in a cold place near the North Pole. Vikings liked to make things from wood, wool and metal.

They were also good farmers and explorers. Sometimes Vikings went a long way in boats to find new places.

village

Viking boats were called longships. Longships were made from wood and had a big sail. They were very fast.

longships

Vikings used the sun, stars and birds to help them find their way.
The Vikings could row their longships right up onto a beach.

warriors

The word Viking means "raider". Sometimes when Vikings came to a new place they took what they wanted.

They were after gold, silver and glass. They also wanted people who they could use as slaves. The Vikings had lots of fights in these new places.

The Vikings were good at fighting. They had helmets, swords, spears and shields to help them.

helmets

Their shields were round and made of wood and metal. The Vikings also used bows and arrows.

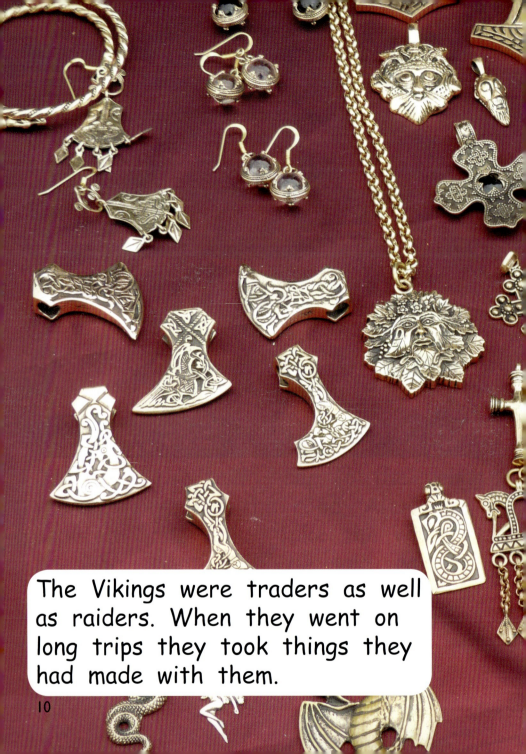

The Vikings were traders as well as raiders. When they went on long trips they took things they had made with them.

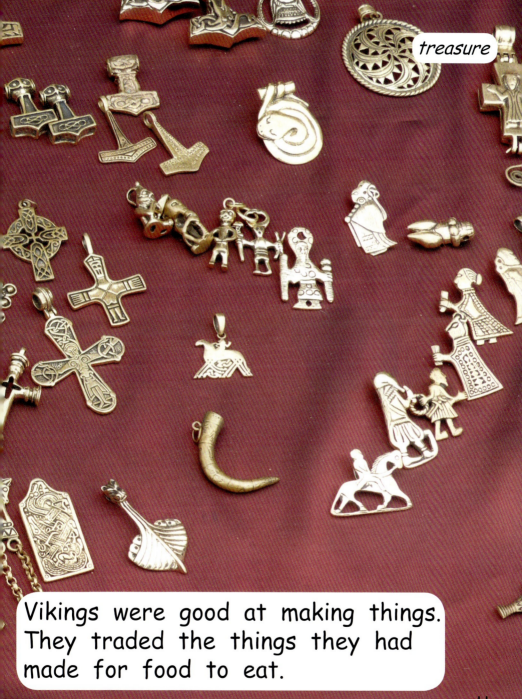

treasure

Vikings were good at making things. They traded the things they had made for food to eat.

Viking families and their animals lived together in homes made of wood, grass or stone. There was one big room with a fire in the middle.

home

In winter, in the afternoons and at night, everyone stayed inside and sat around the fire. They sang songs, told stories, said poems and played board games.

In summer, everyone stayed outside. They played ball games and swam in the sea. The Vikings told stories — many Viking stories were about their gods.

Vikings had many gods. The one everyone knows best is Thor, the god of thunder. Thor had magic gloves, a magic belt and a hammer. He looked after the Vikings.